THE BEATLES
FOR FOLK HARP
22 CLASSICS ARRANGED FOR FOLK HARP

Arranged by Maeve Gilchrist

ISBN 978-1-4584-0761-0

Hal•Leonard®
CORPORATION
7777 W. BLUEMOUND RD. P.O. BOX 13819 MILWAUKEE, WI 53213

Visit Hal Leonard Online at
www.halleonard.com

Across the Universe

Words and Music by John Lennon and Paul McCartney

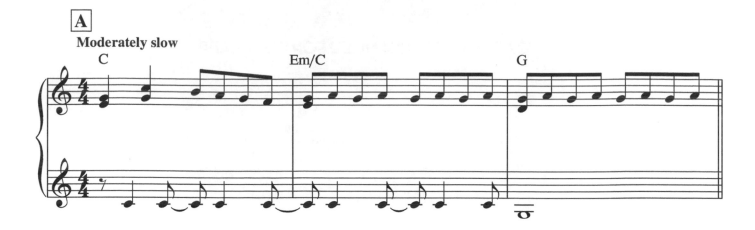

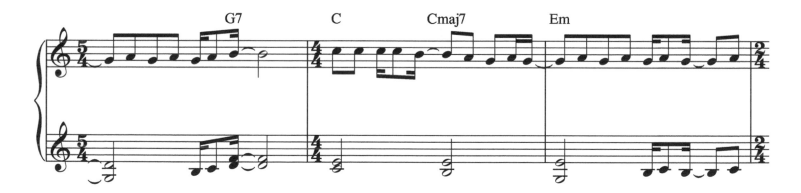

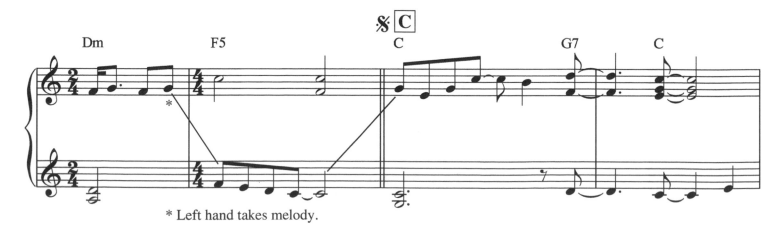

* Left hand takes melody.

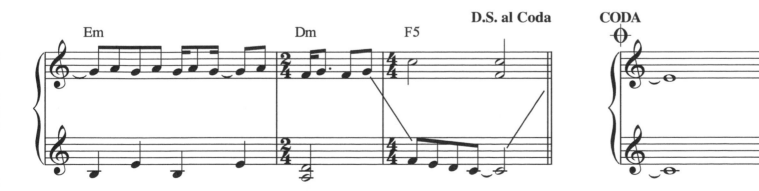

Act Naturally

Words and Music by Vonie Morrison and Johnny Russell

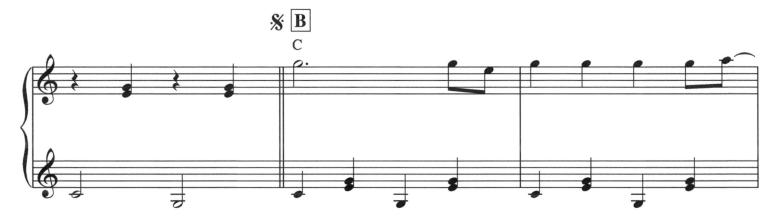

To Coda ⊕

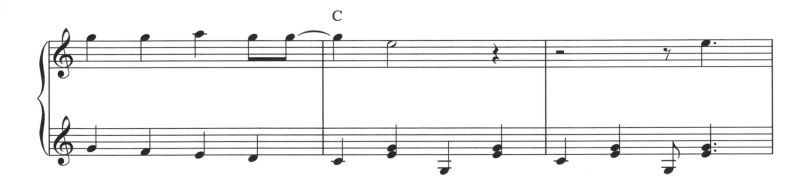

6

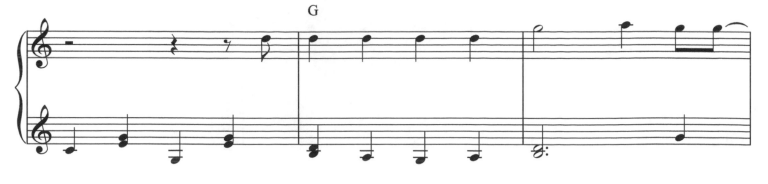

D.S. al Coda

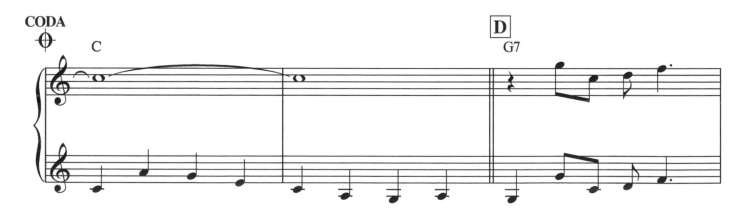

All Together Now

Words and Music by John Lennon and Paul McCartney

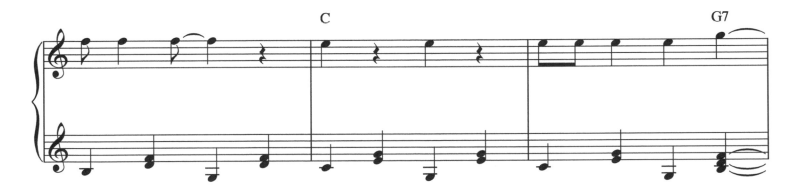

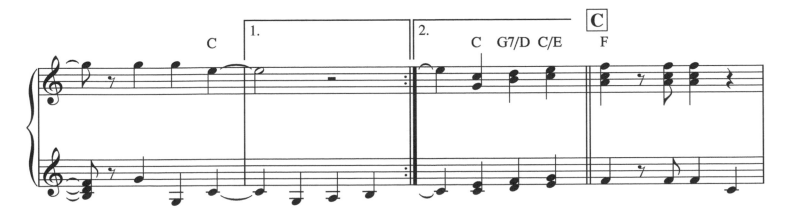

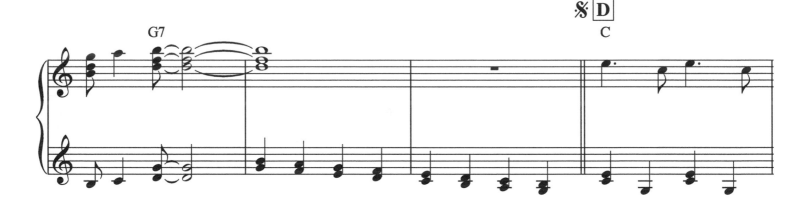

D.S. al Coda

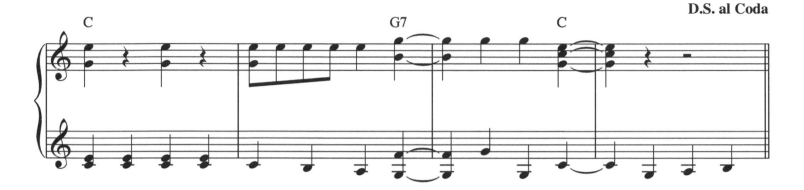

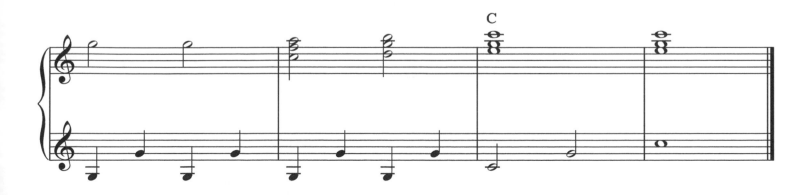

And I Love Her

Words and Music by John Lennon and Paul McCartney

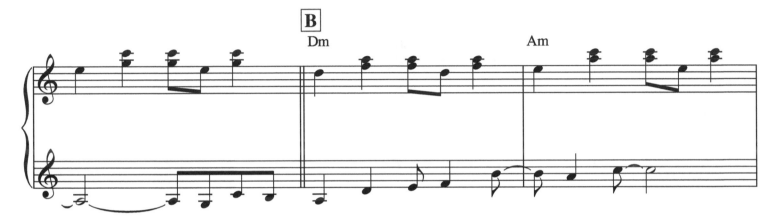

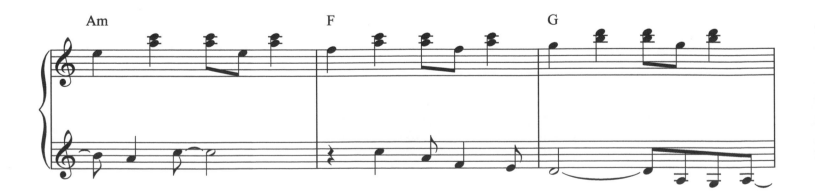

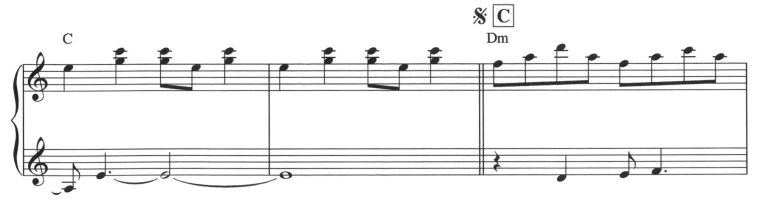

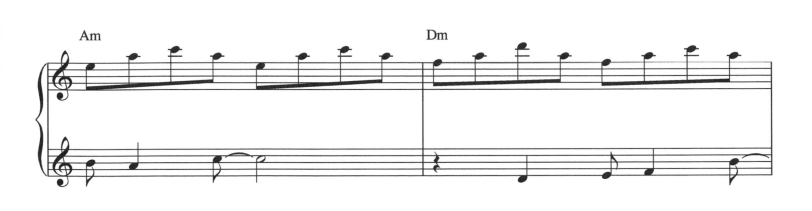

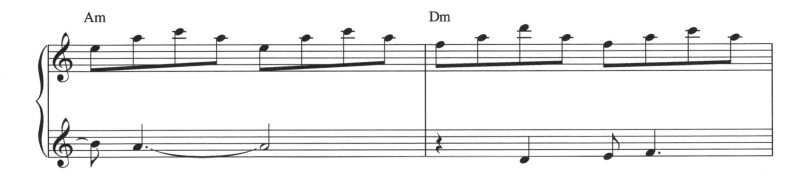

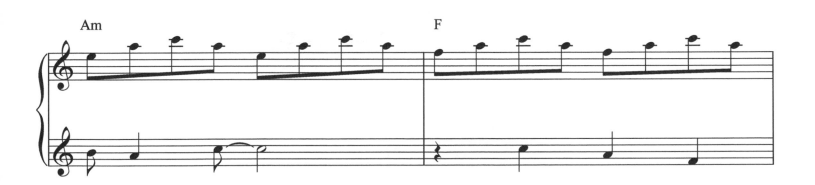

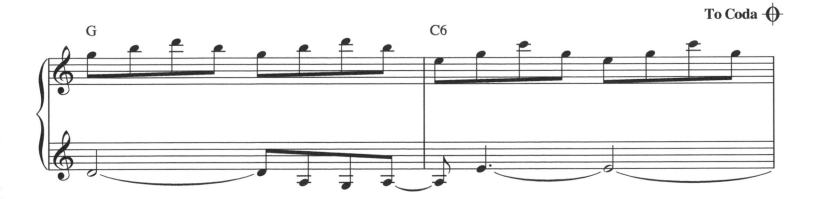

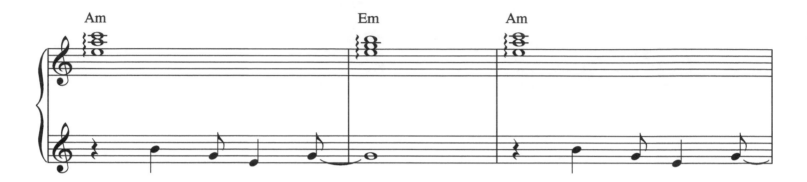

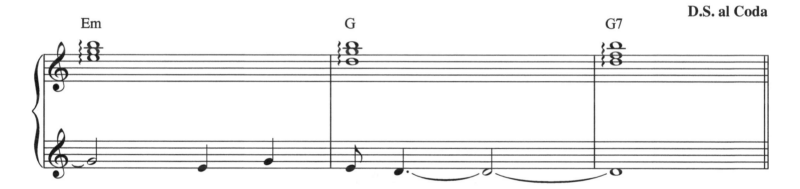

D.S. al Coda

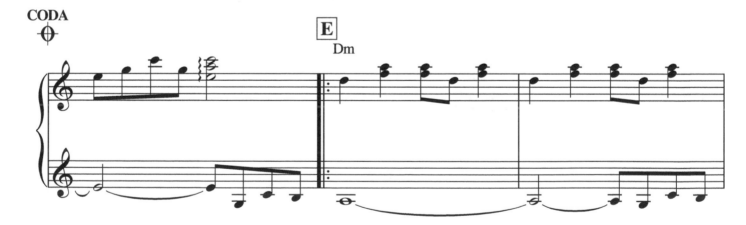

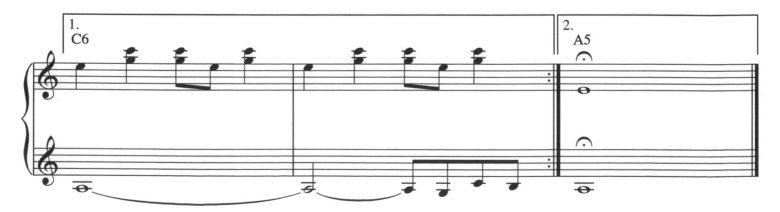

Don't Let Me Down

Words and Music by John Lennon and Paul McCartney

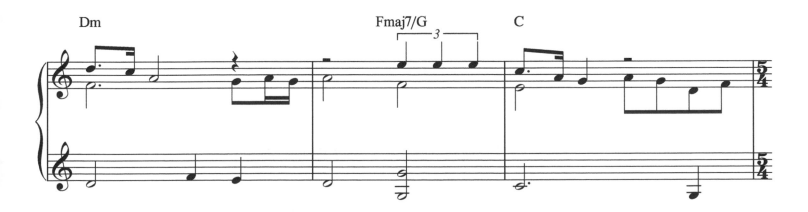

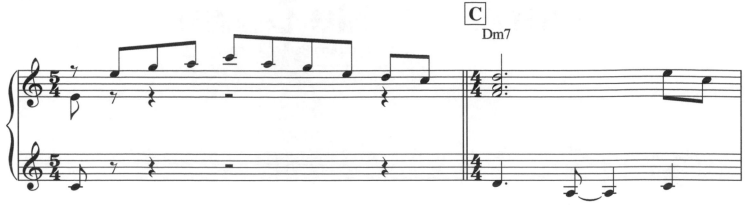

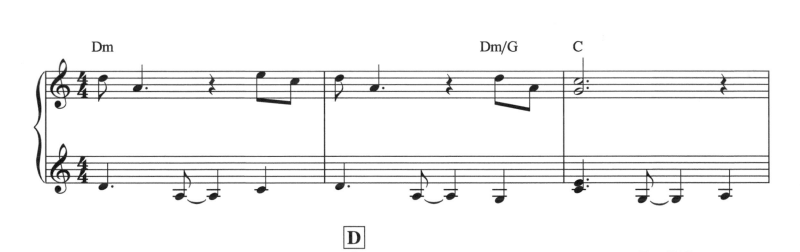

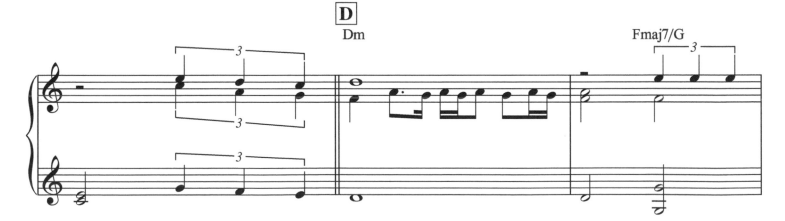

Eight Days a Week

Words and Music by John Lennon and Paul McCartney

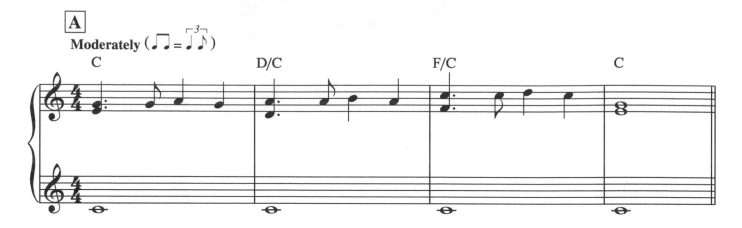

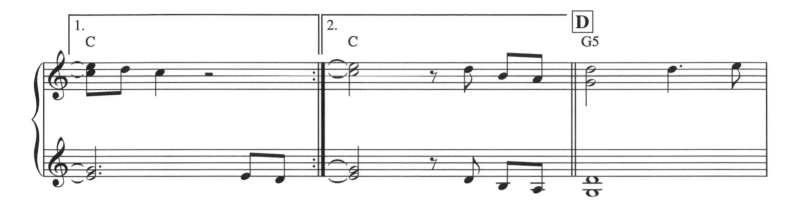

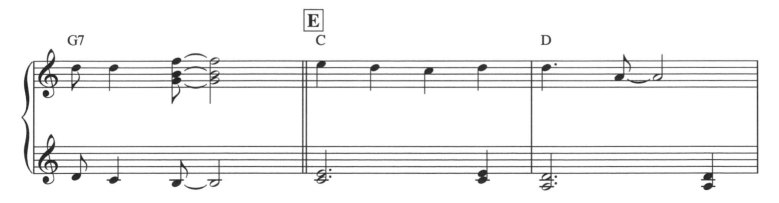

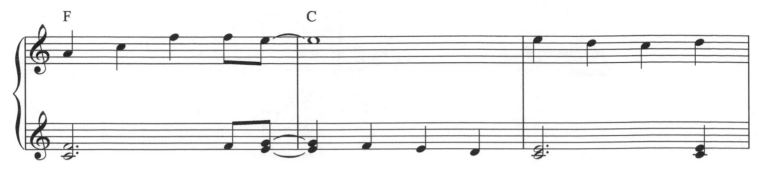

D.S. al Coda

CODA

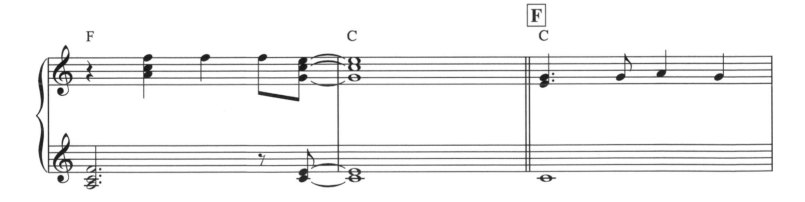

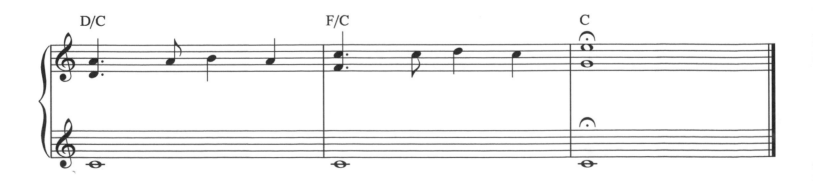

Help!

Words and Music by John Lennon and Paul McCartney

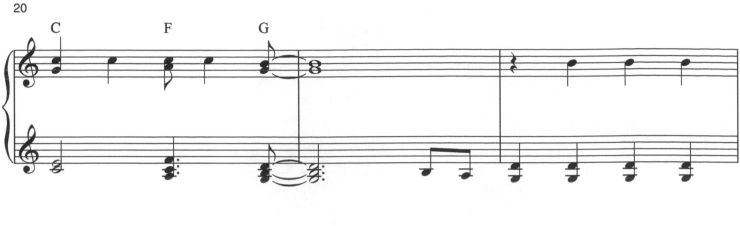

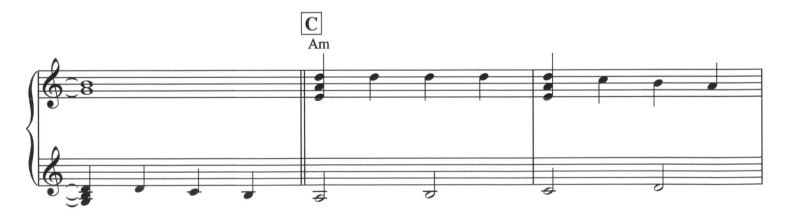

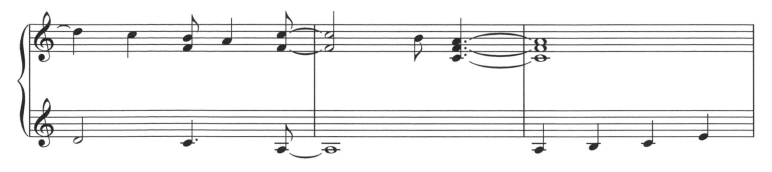

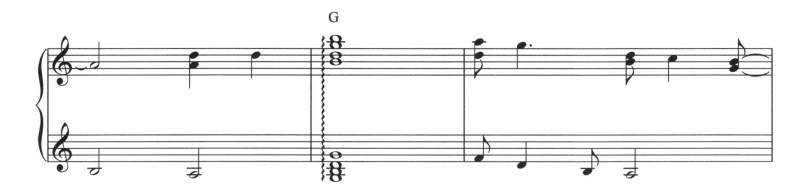

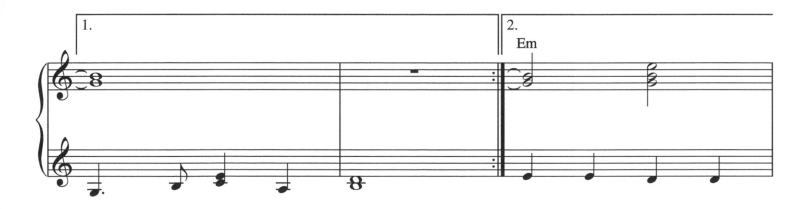

Golden Slumbers

Words and Music by John Lennon and Paul McCartney

Moderately

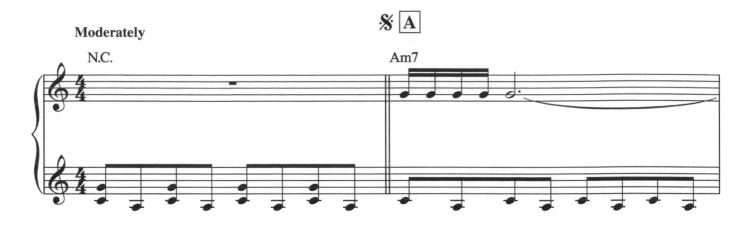

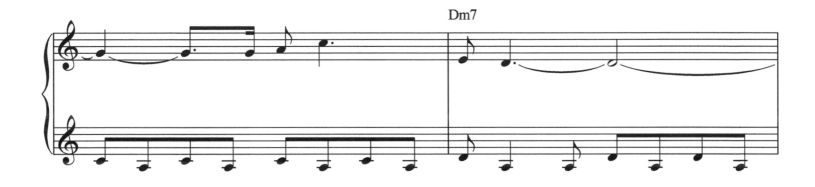

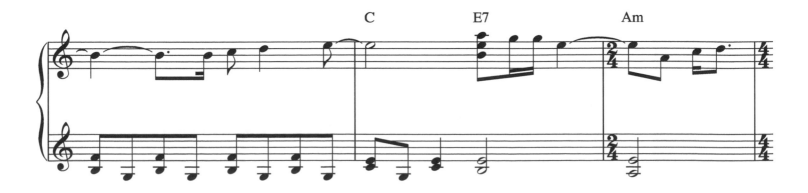

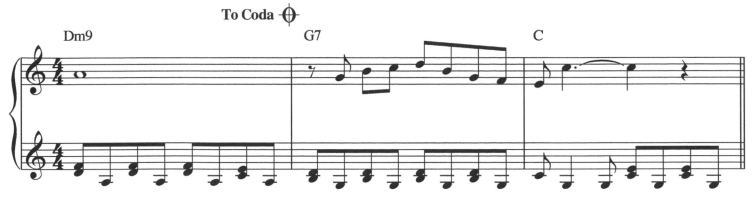

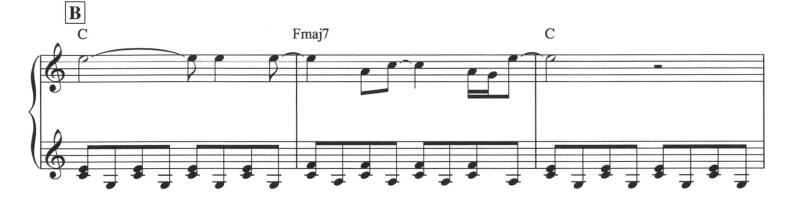

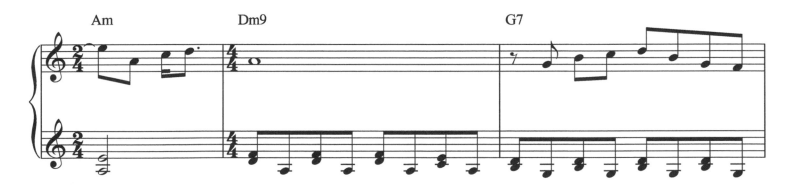

Good Night

Words and Music by John Lennon and Paul McCartney

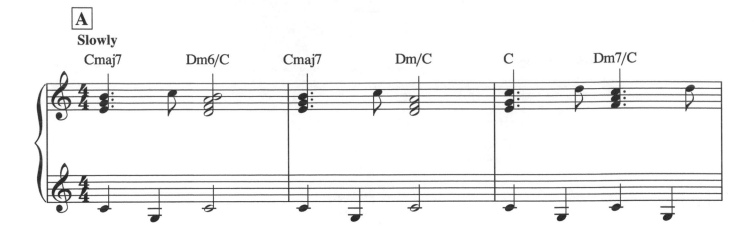

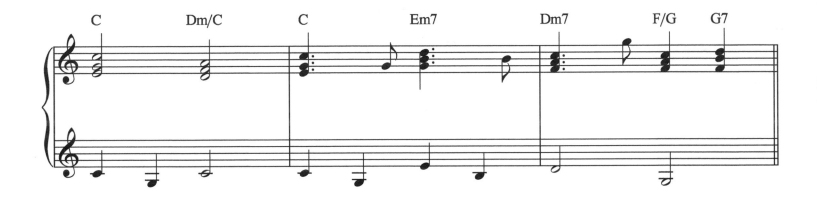

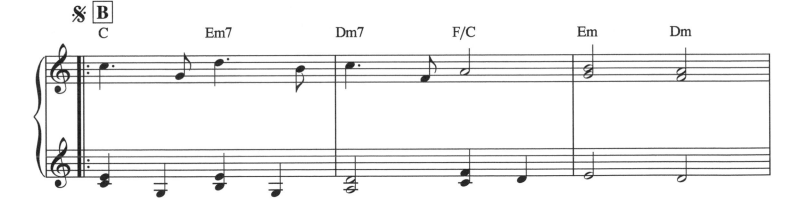

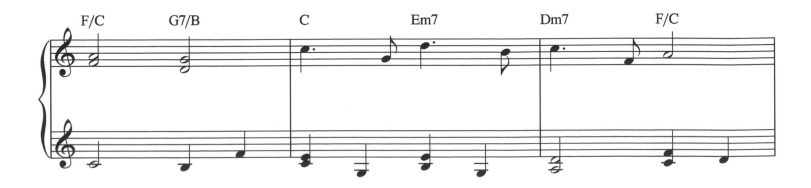

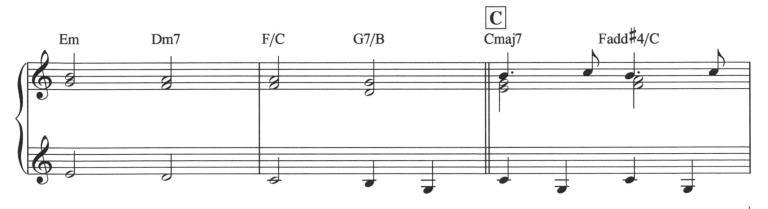

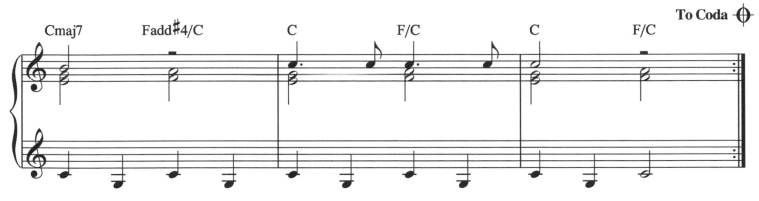

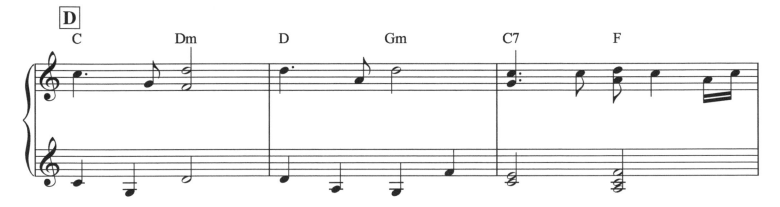

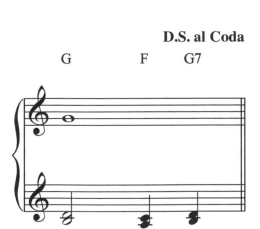

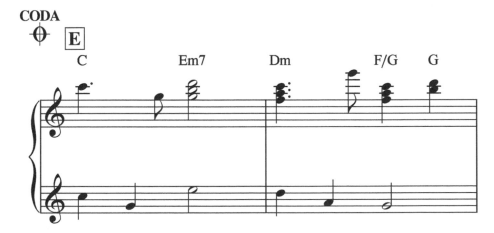

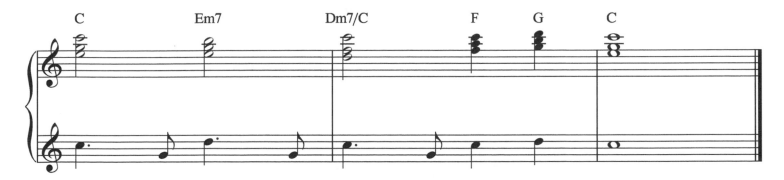

I'm a Loser

Words and Music by John Lennon and Paul McCartney

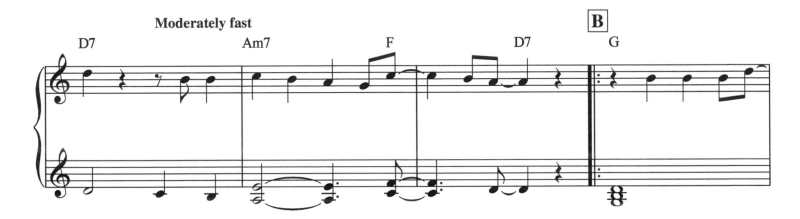

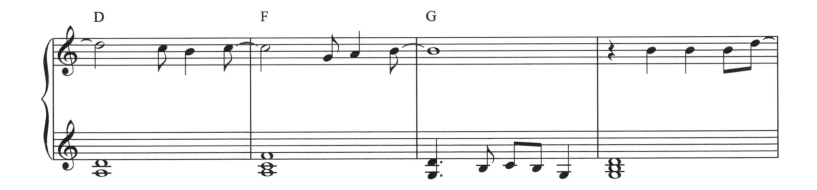

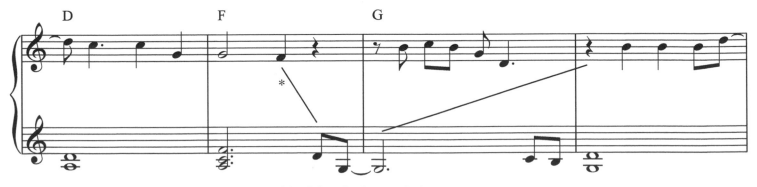

* Left hand takes melody.

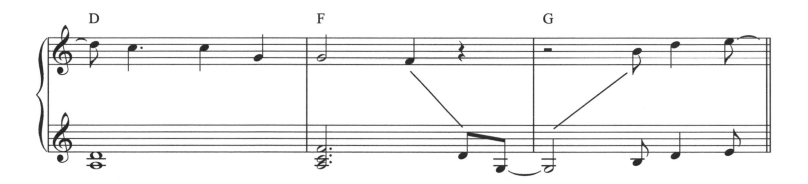

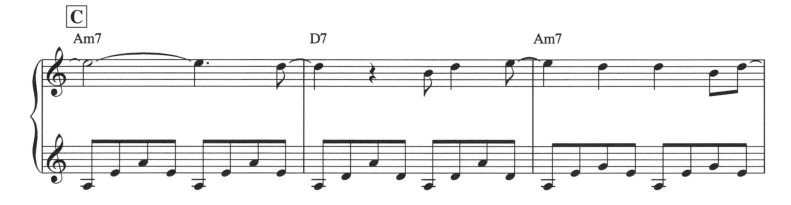

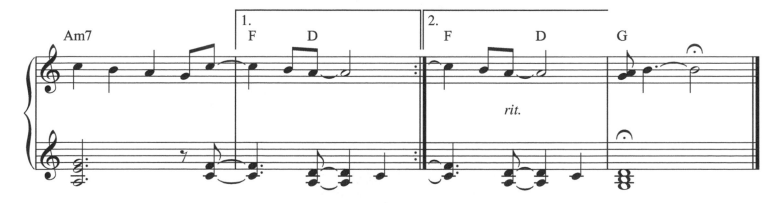

I've Just Seen a Face

Words and Music by John Lennon and Paul McCartney

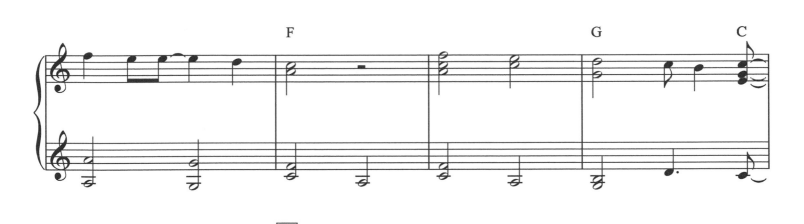

30

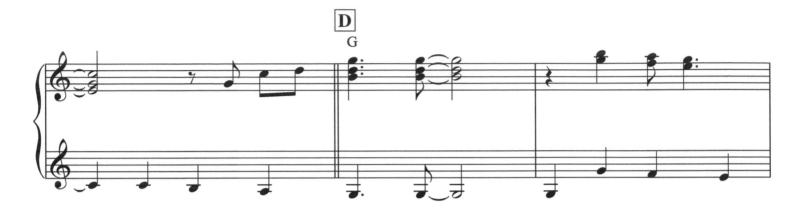

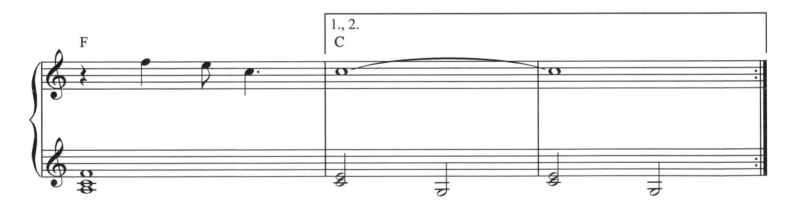

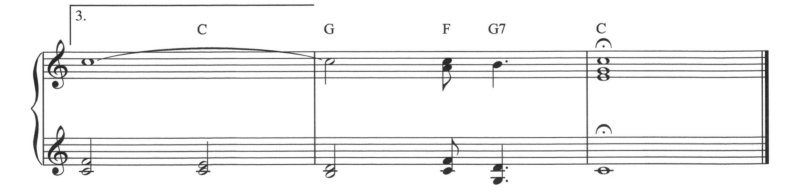

Let It Be

Words and Music by John Lennon and Paul McCartney

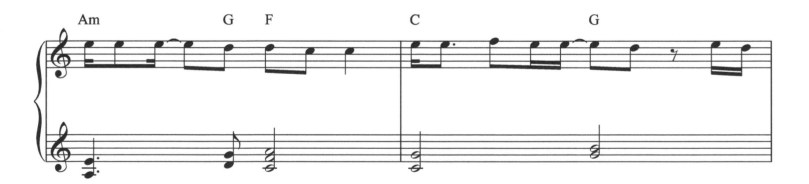

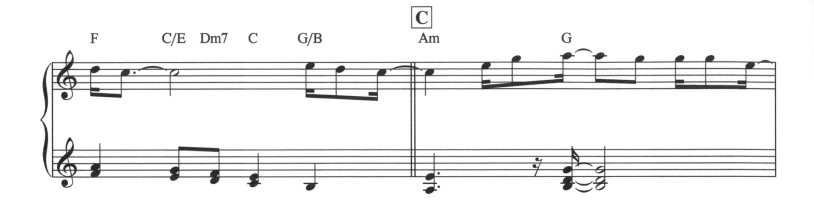

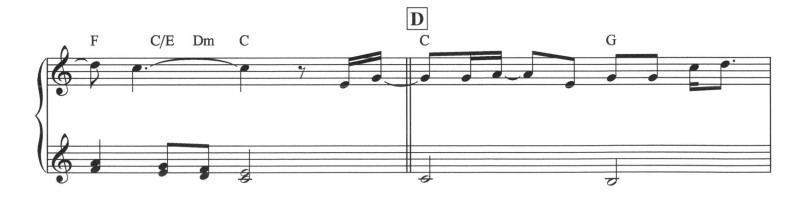

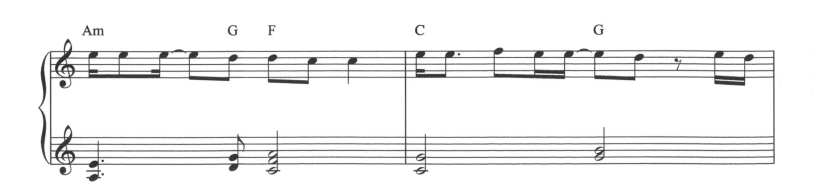

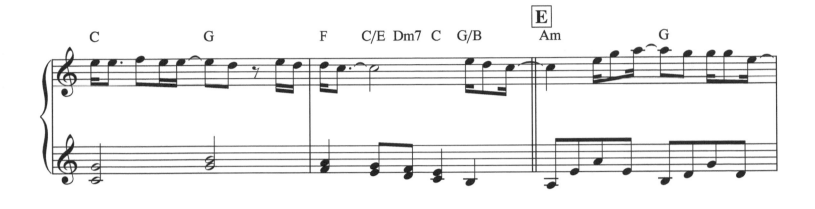

Ob-La-Di, Ob-La-Da

Words and Music by John Lennon and Paul McCartney

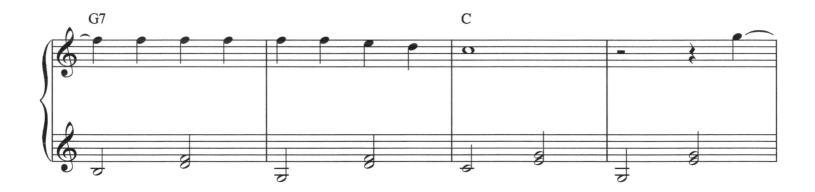

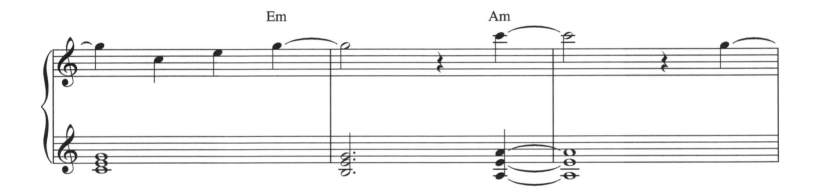

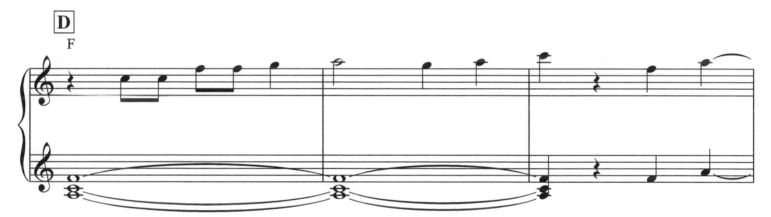

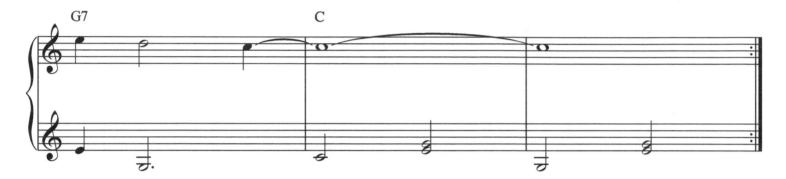

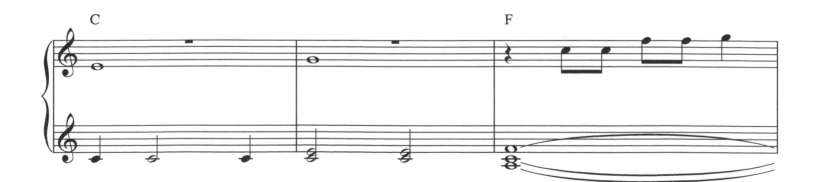

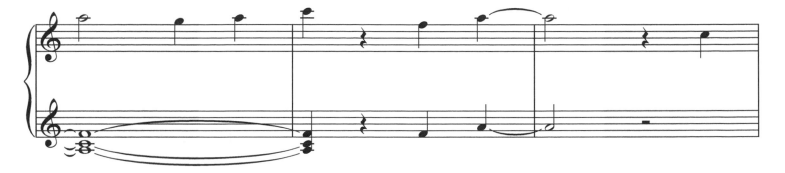

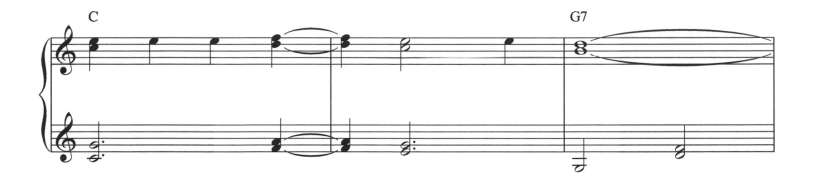

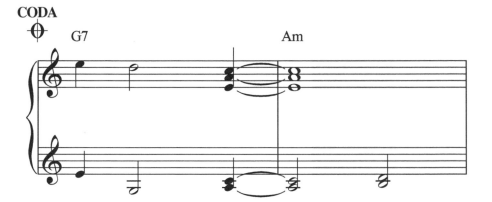

D.S. al Coda

CODA

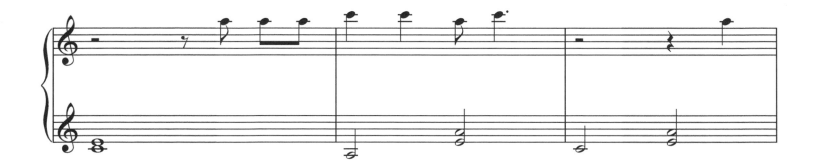

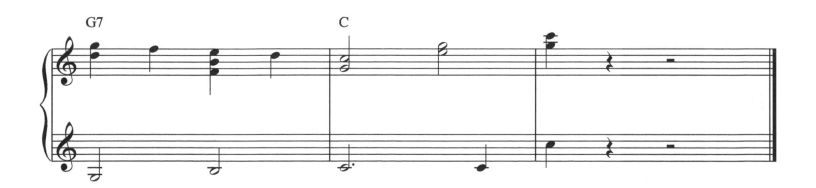

Octopus's Garden

Words and Music by Richard Starkey, John Lennon and Paul McCartney

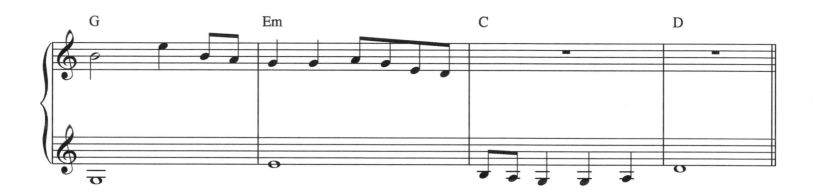

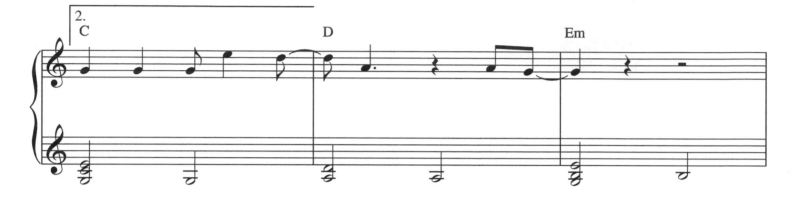

Paperback Writer

Words and Music by John Lennon and Paul McCartney

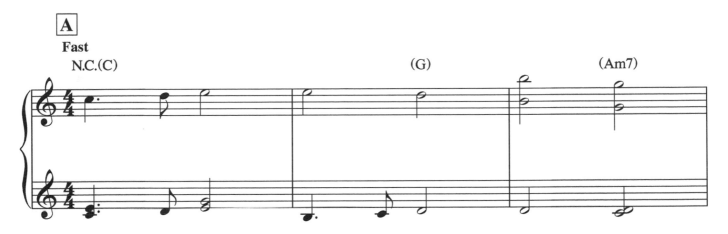

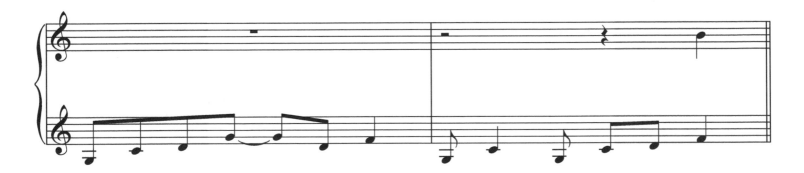

C

1., 3.
G7

2., 4.
G7

Please Mr. Postman

Words and Music by Robert Bateman, Georgia Dobbins, William Garrett,
Freddie Gorman and Brian Holland

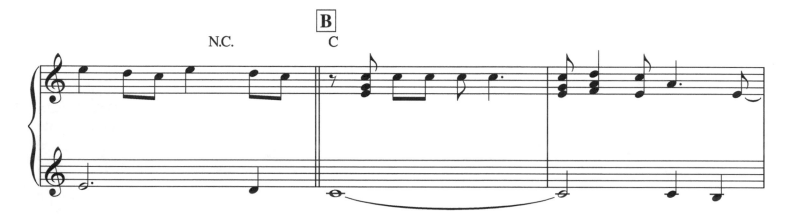

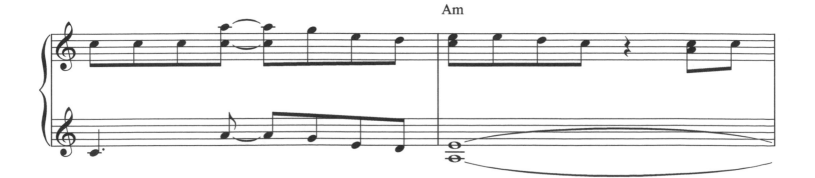

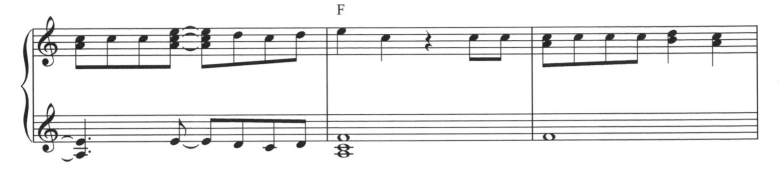

Please Please Me

Words and Music by John Lennon and Paul McCartney

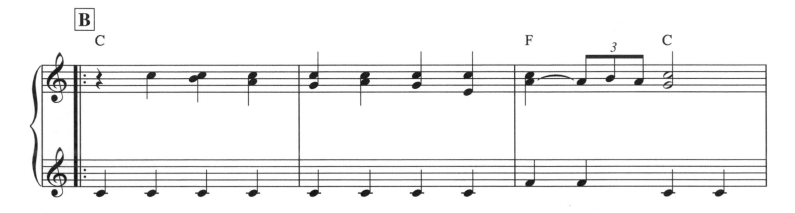

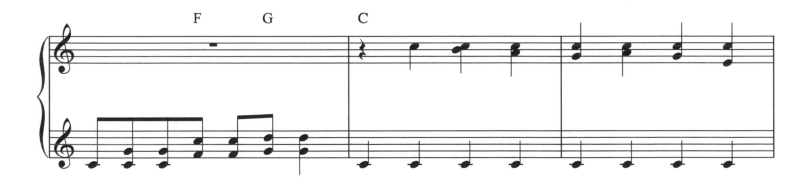

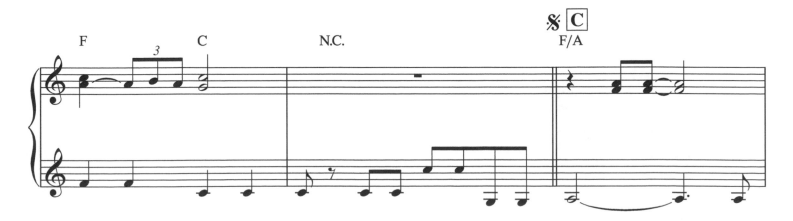

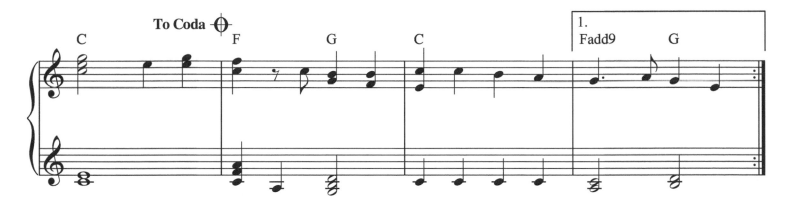

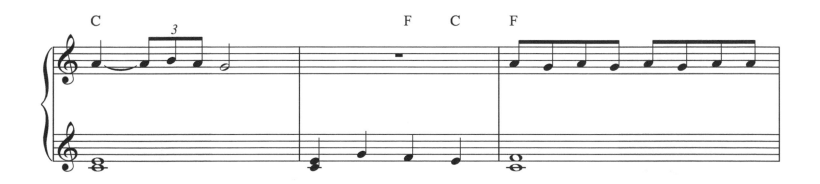

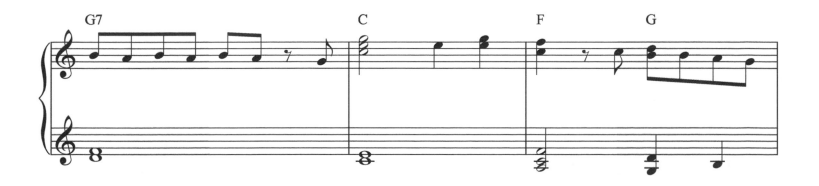

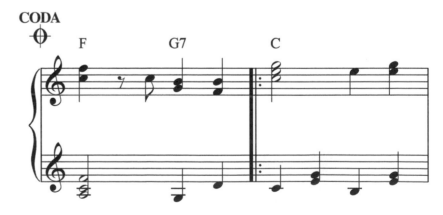

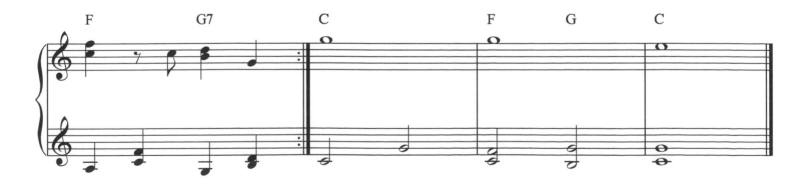

Rain

Words and Music by John Lennon and Paul McCartney

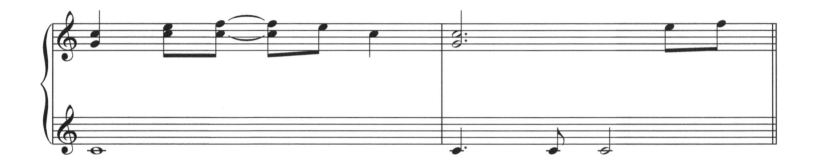

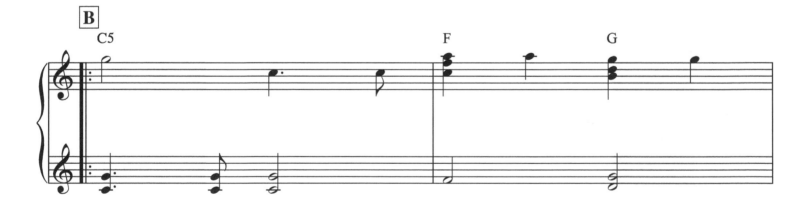

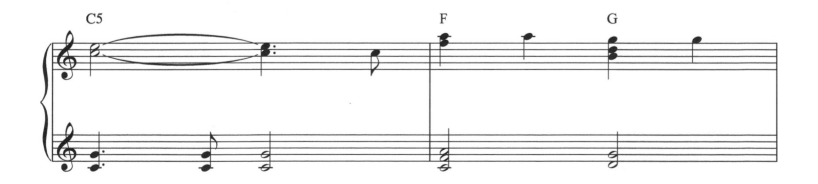

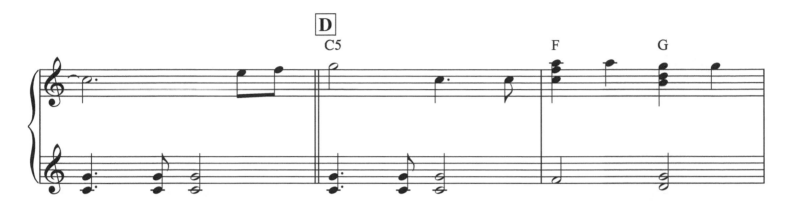

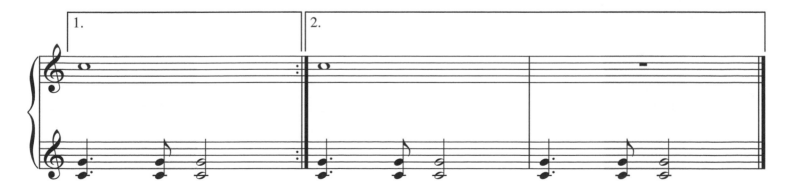

Rocky Raccoon

Words and Music by John Lennon and Paul McCartney

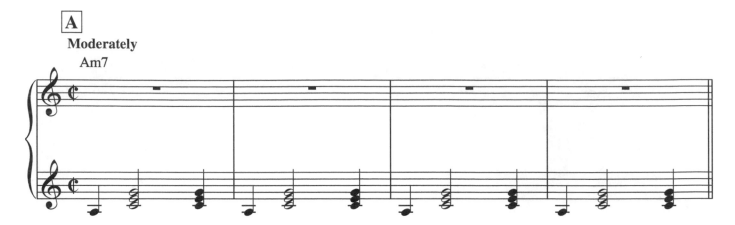

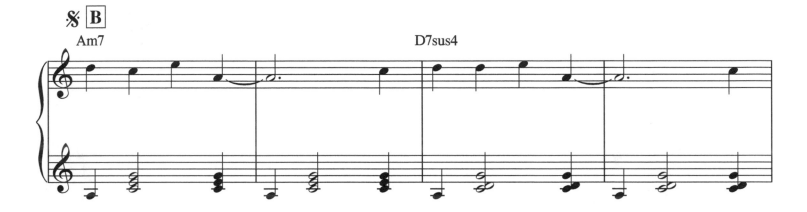

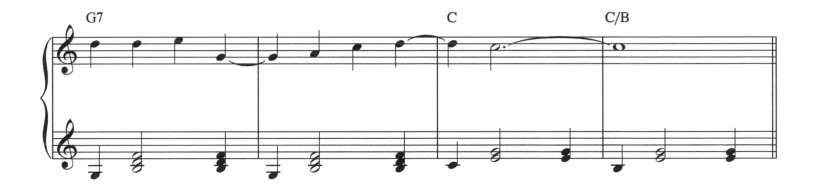

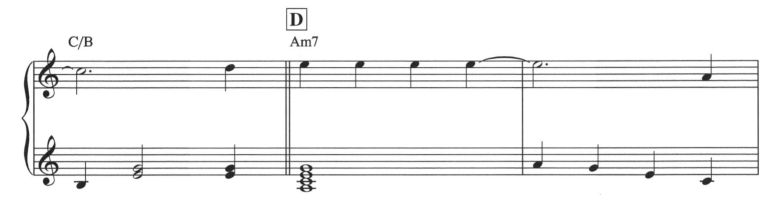

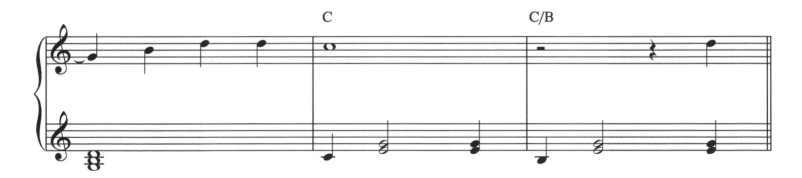

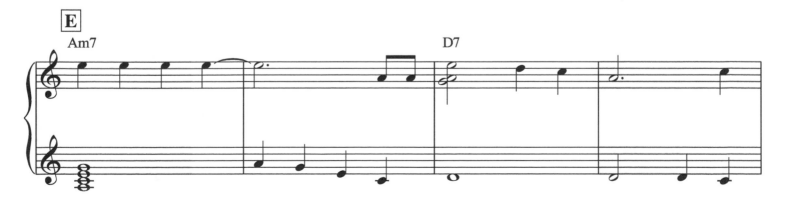

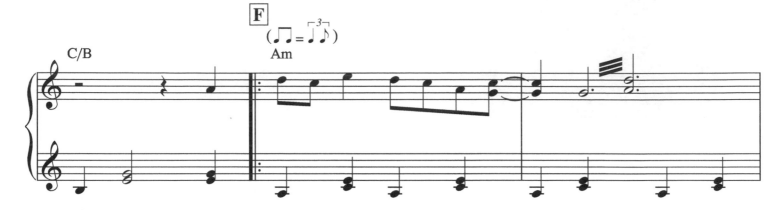

* Left hand momentarily takes melody.

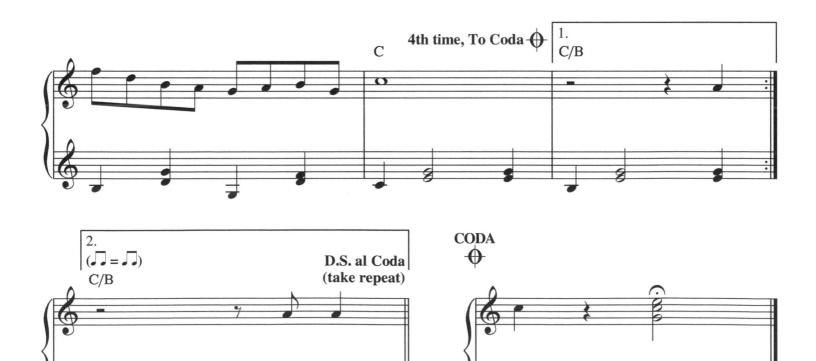

Twist and Shout

Words and Music by Bert Russell and Phil Medley

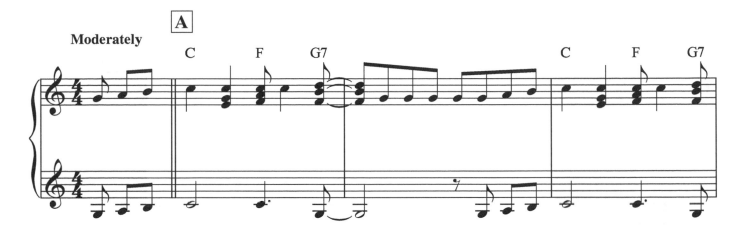

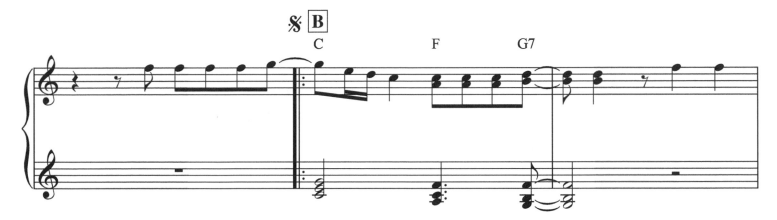

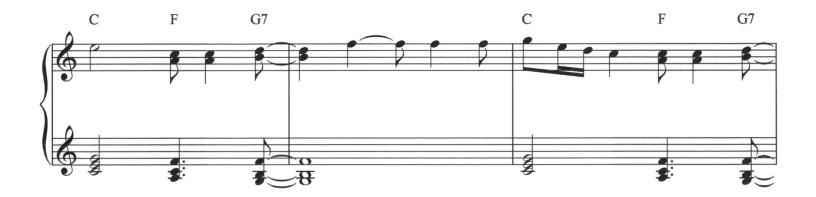

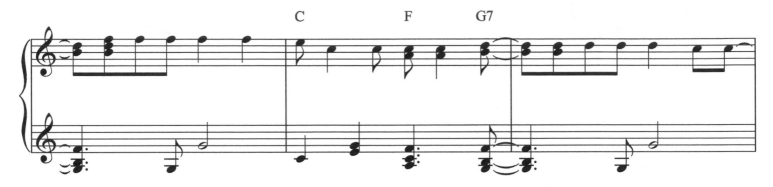

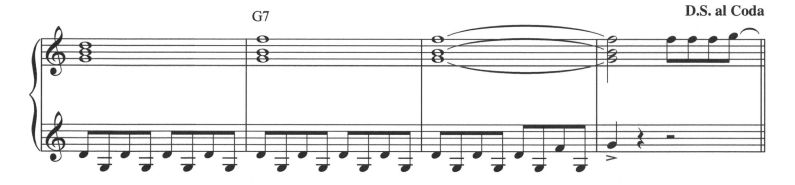

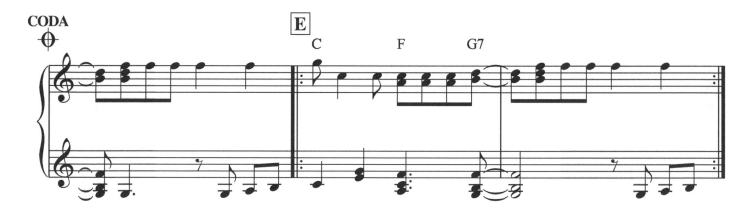

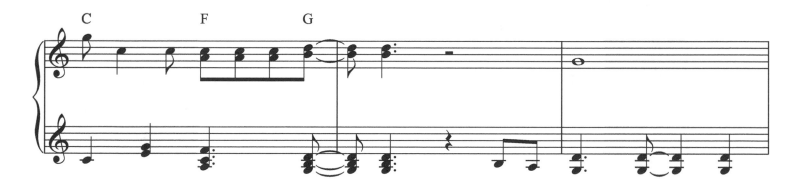

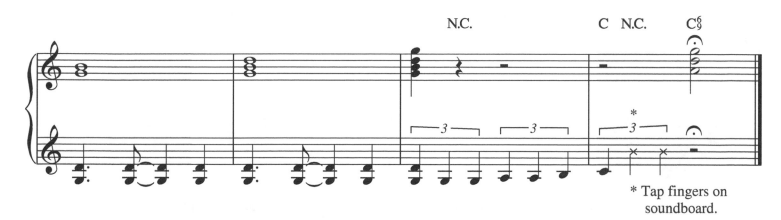

* Tap fingers on
  soundboard.

Tell Me What You See

Words and Music by John Lennon and Paul McCartney

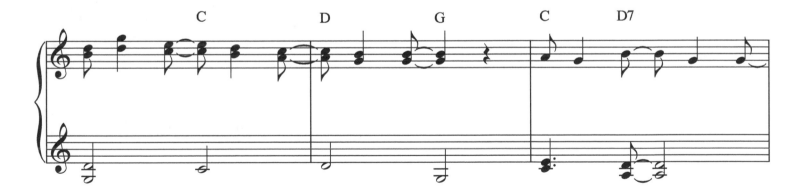

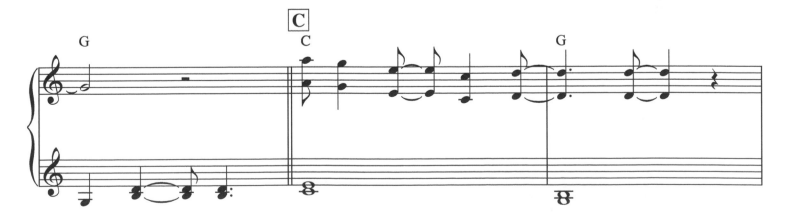

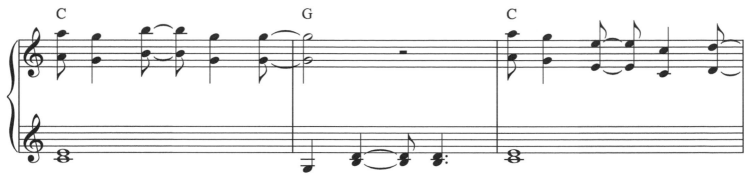

Yellow Submarine

Words and Music by John Lennon and Paul McCartney

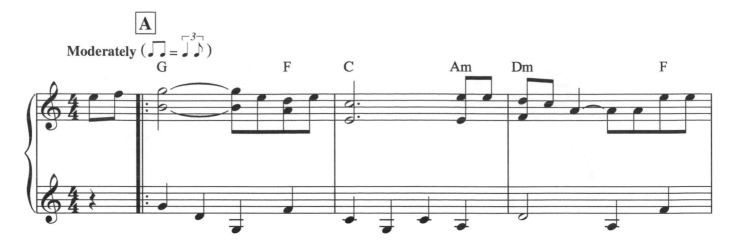

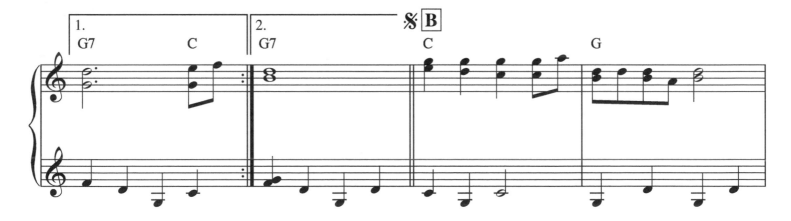

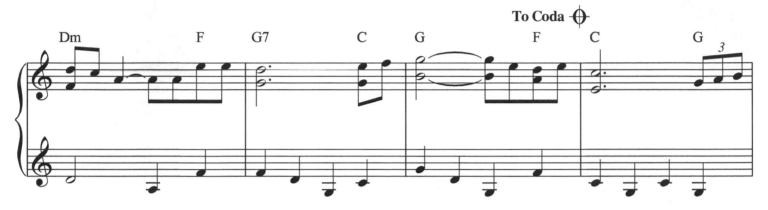

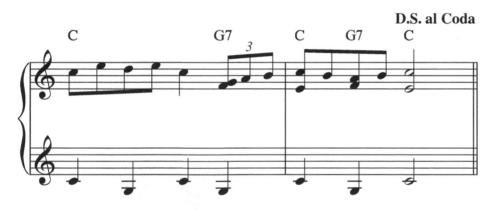
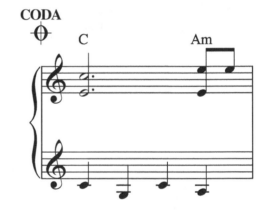

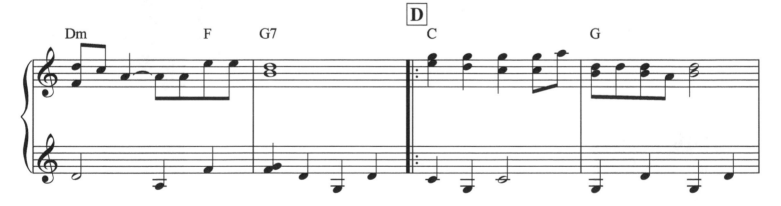

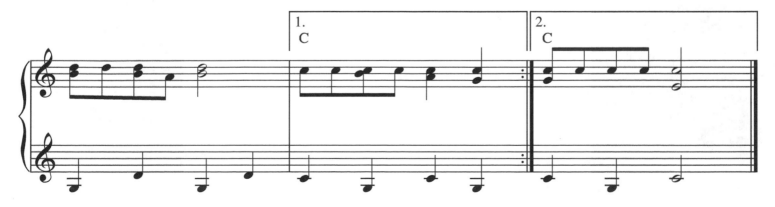